Whispers of Silence

George Digalakis

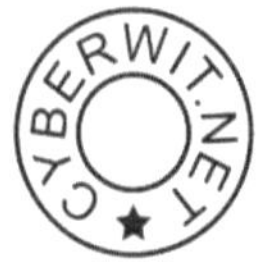

Cyberwit.net
HIG 45 Kaushambi Kunj, Kalindipuram
Allahabad - 211011 (U.P.) India
http://www.cyberwit.net
Tel: +(91) 9415091004 +(91) (532) 2552257
E-mail: info@cyberwit.net

Printed at Thomson Press India Limited.

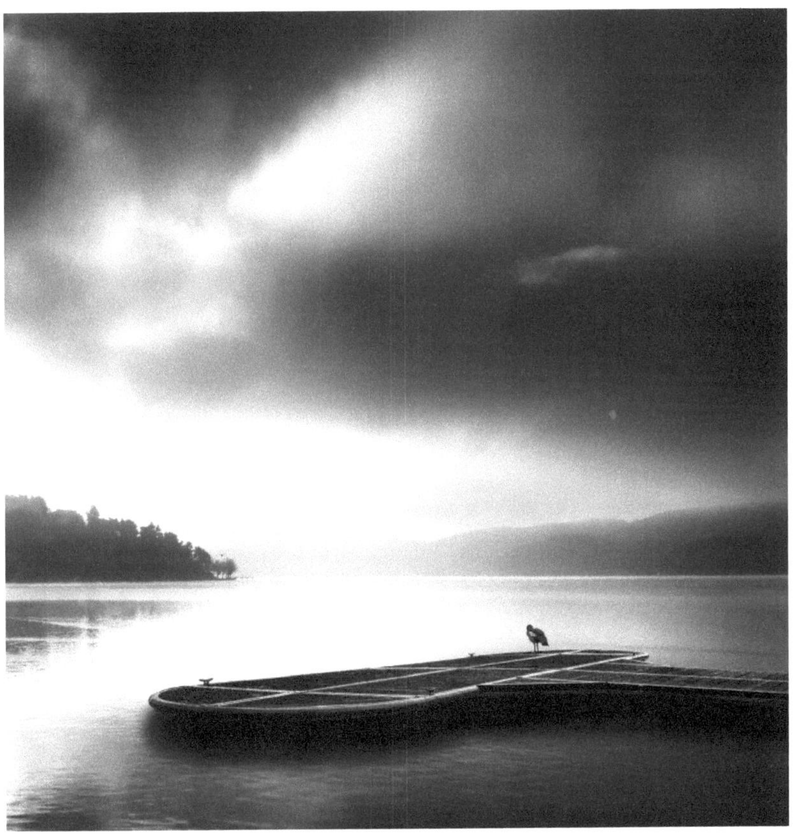

A Place for Meditation

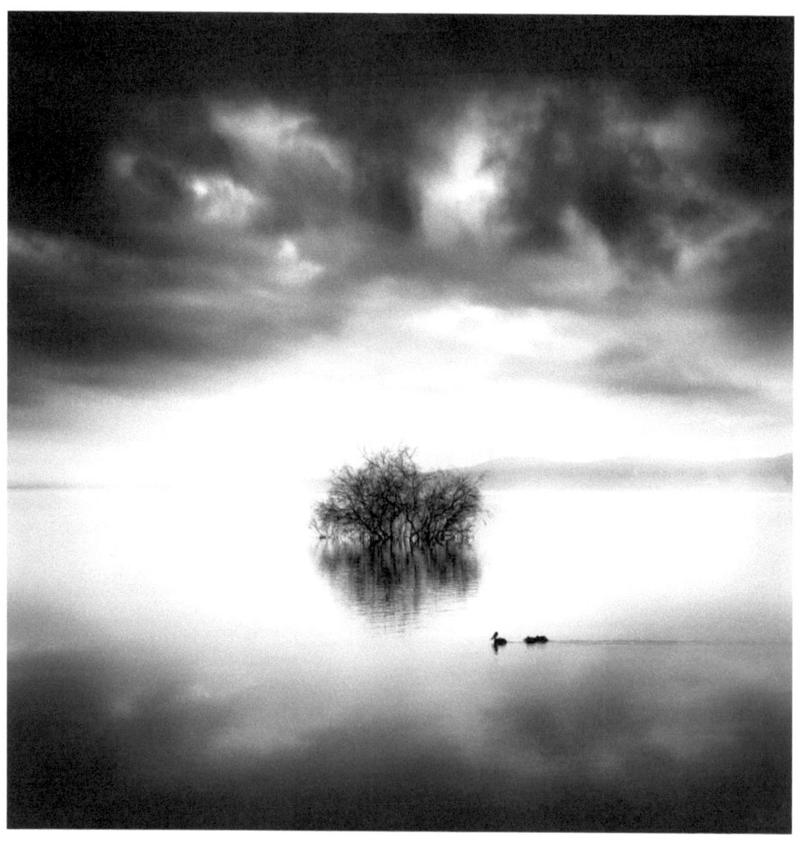

A Ray of Light

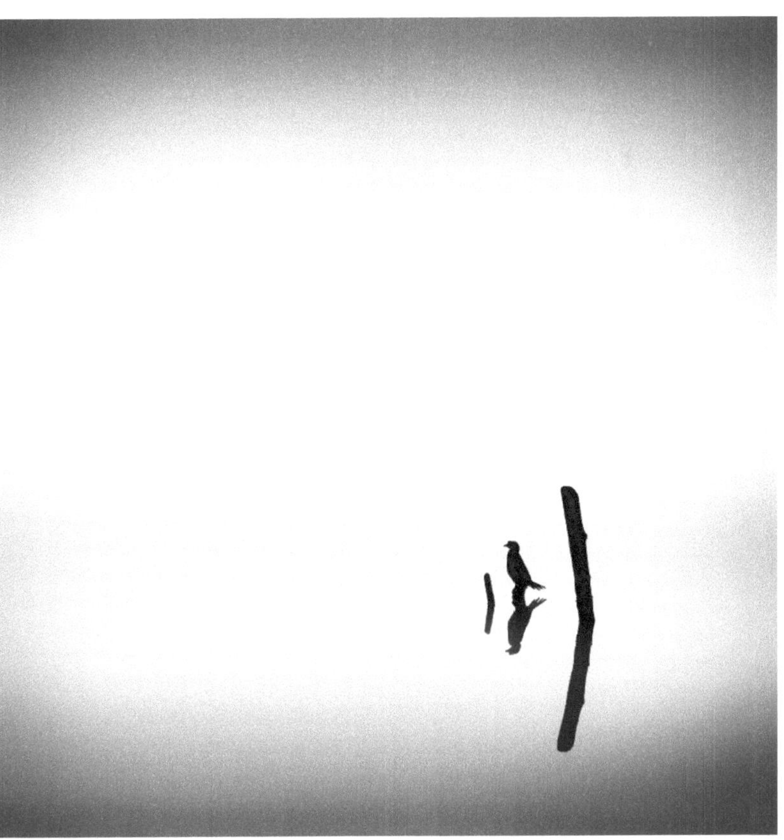

A Whiter Shade of Pale

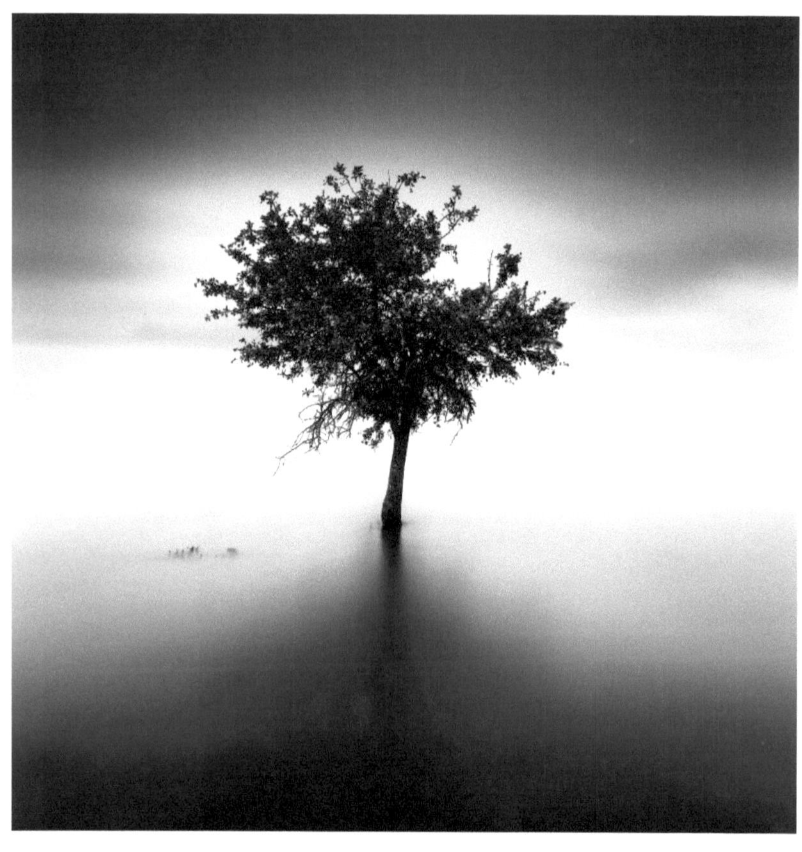

And the New Day will Dawn

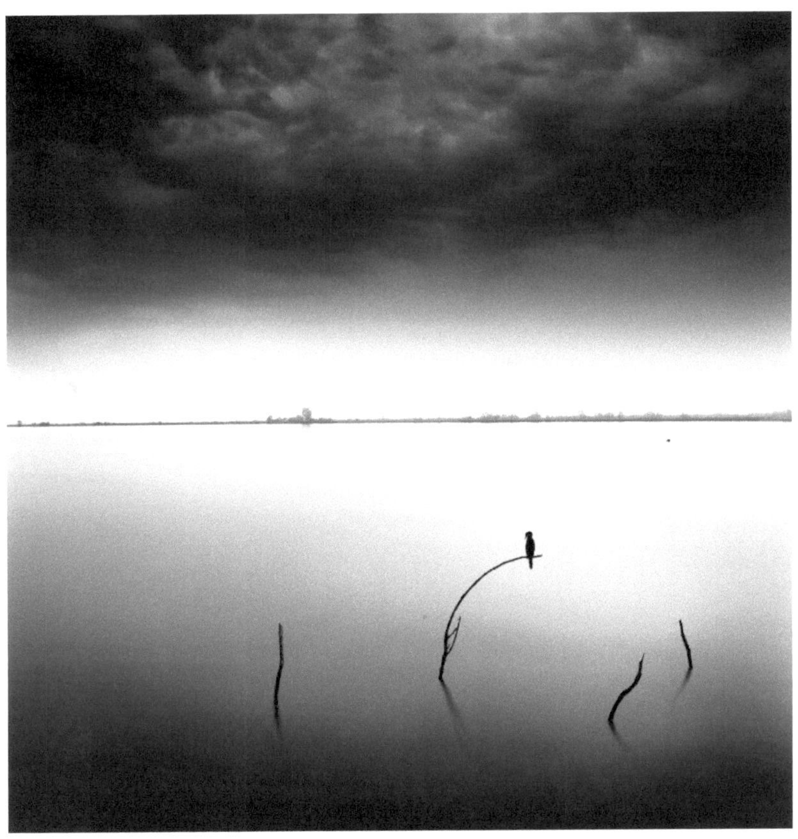

Blackbird

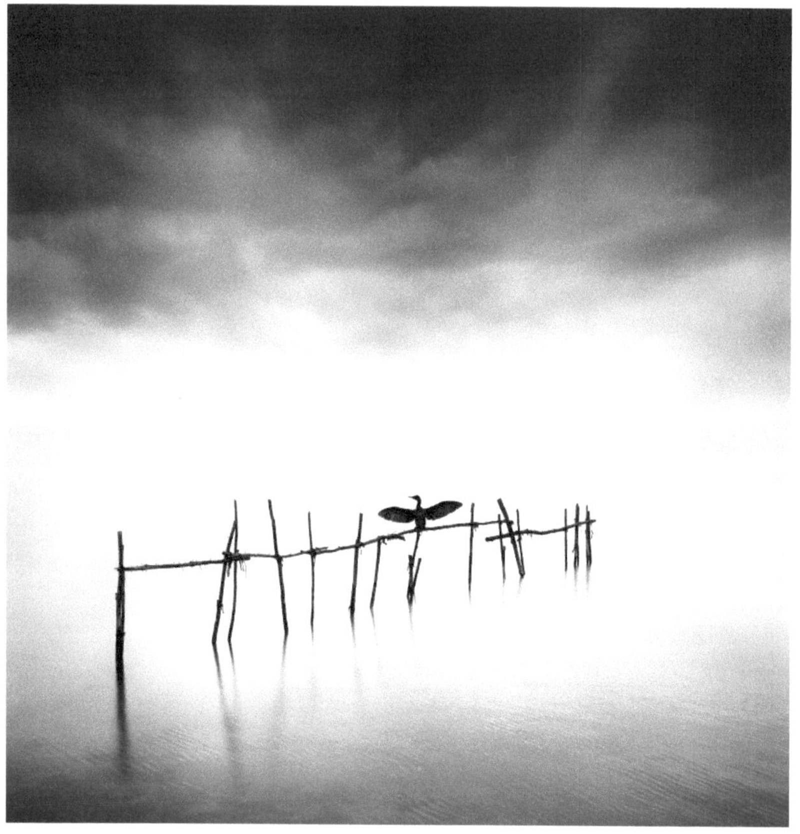

Cormorant

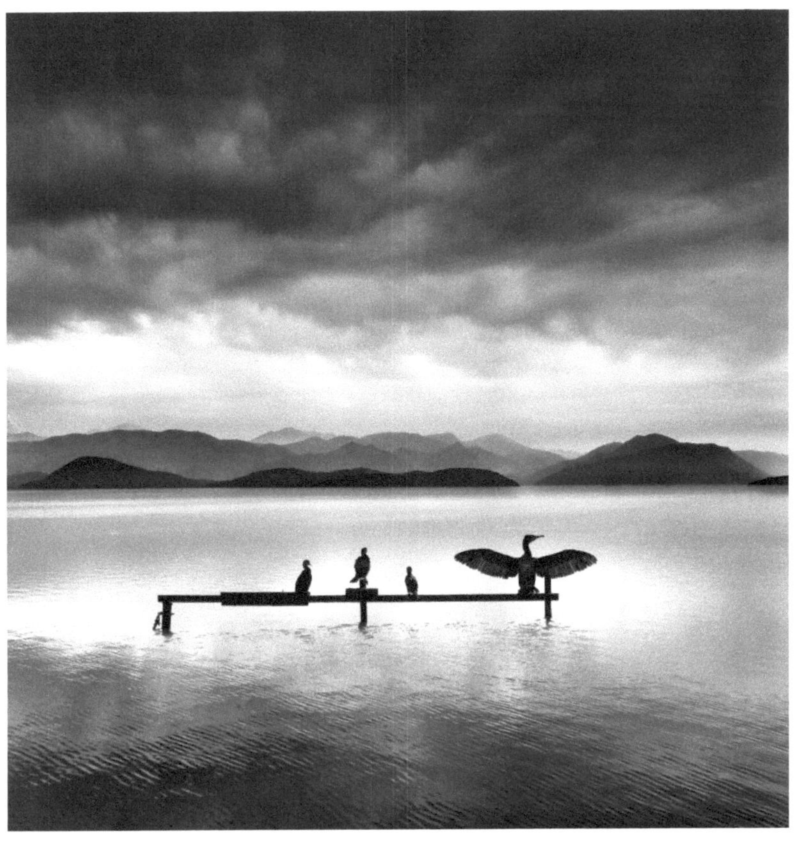

Distant Mountains

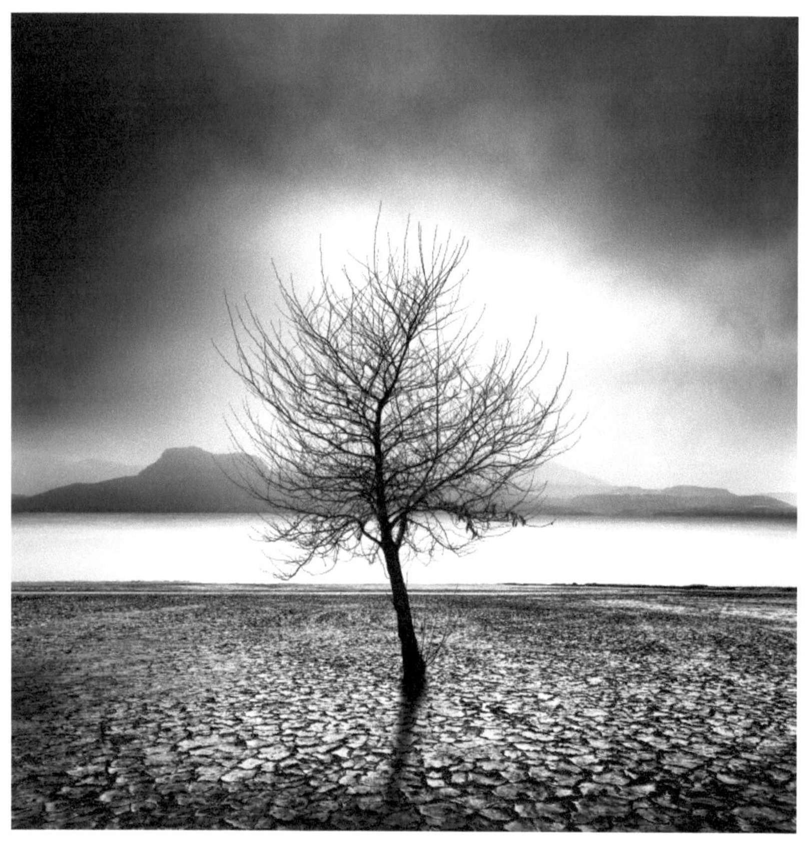

Dry Land

Everything Beautiful Is Far Away

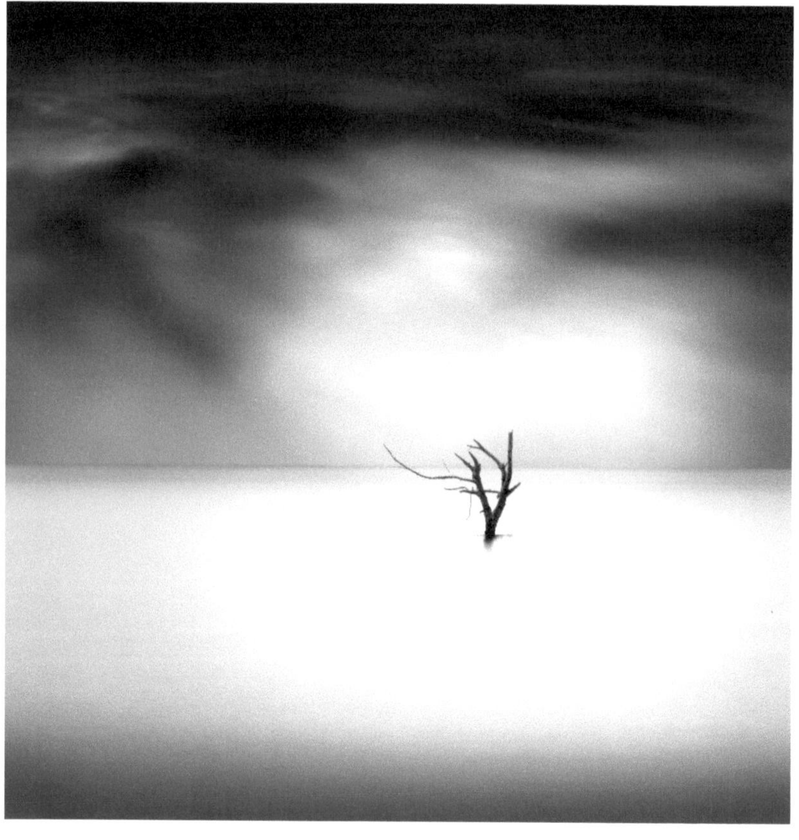

Feel the Silence

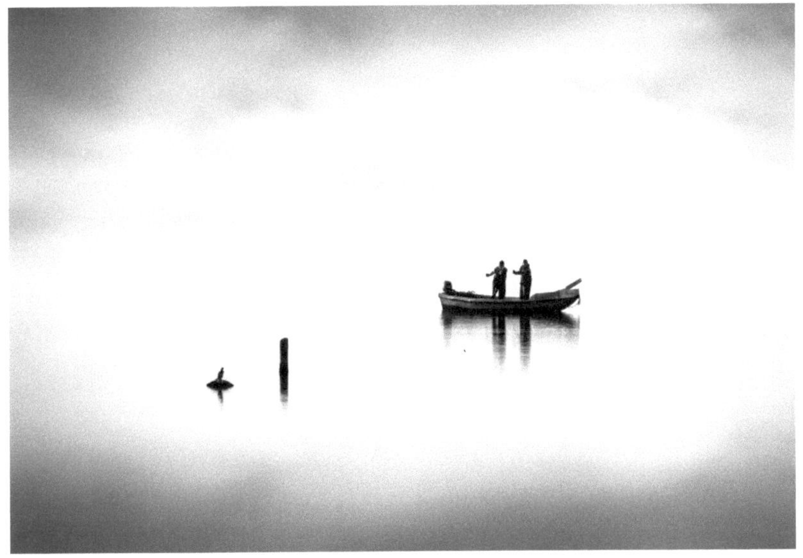

Fishermen and the Curious Bird II

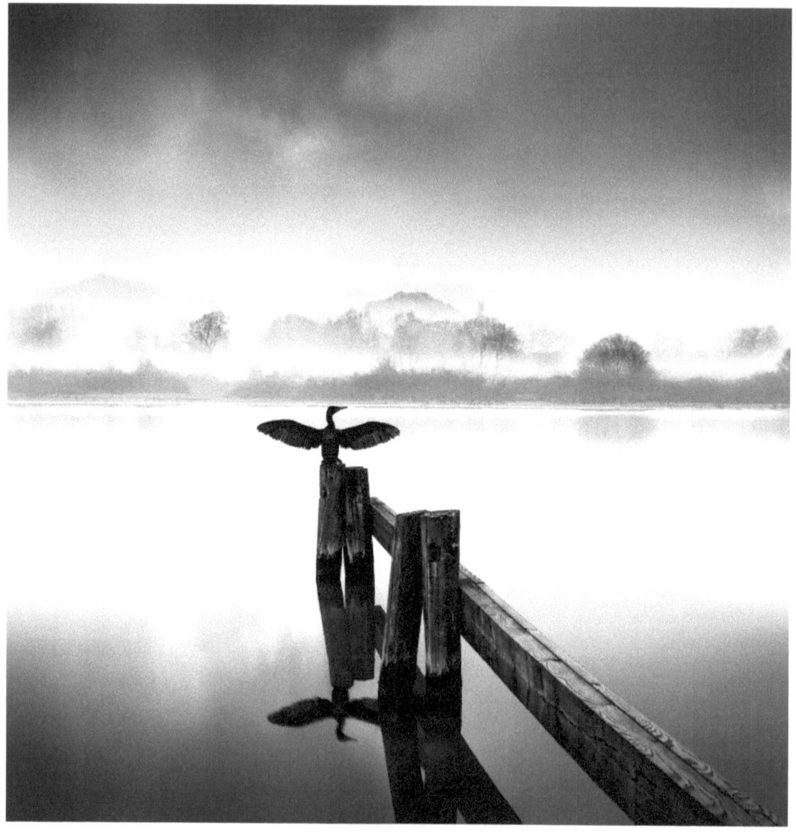

Fly Away

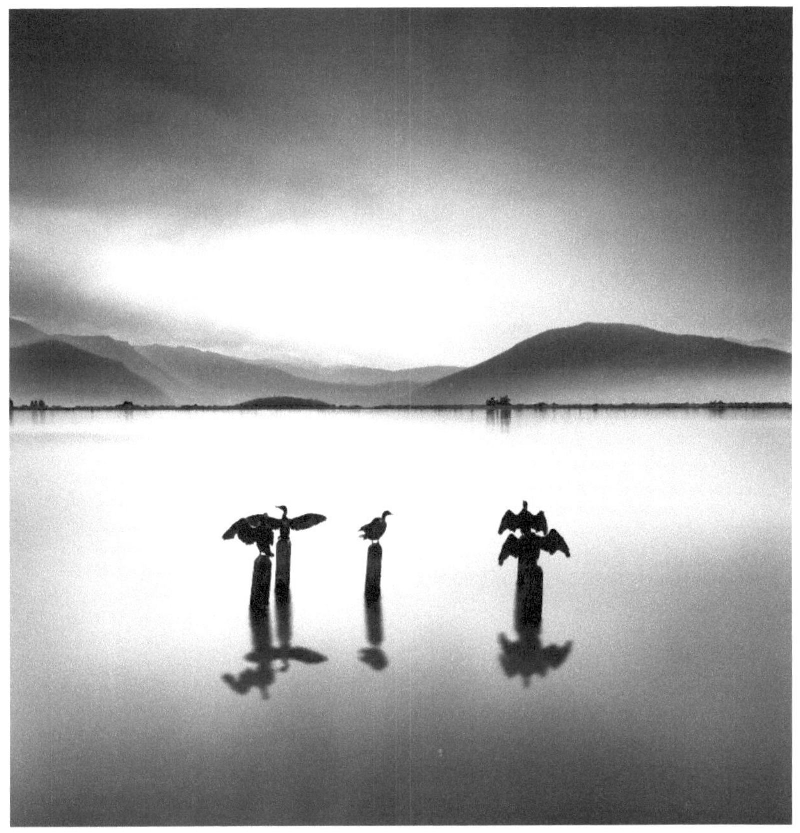

Fully Booked

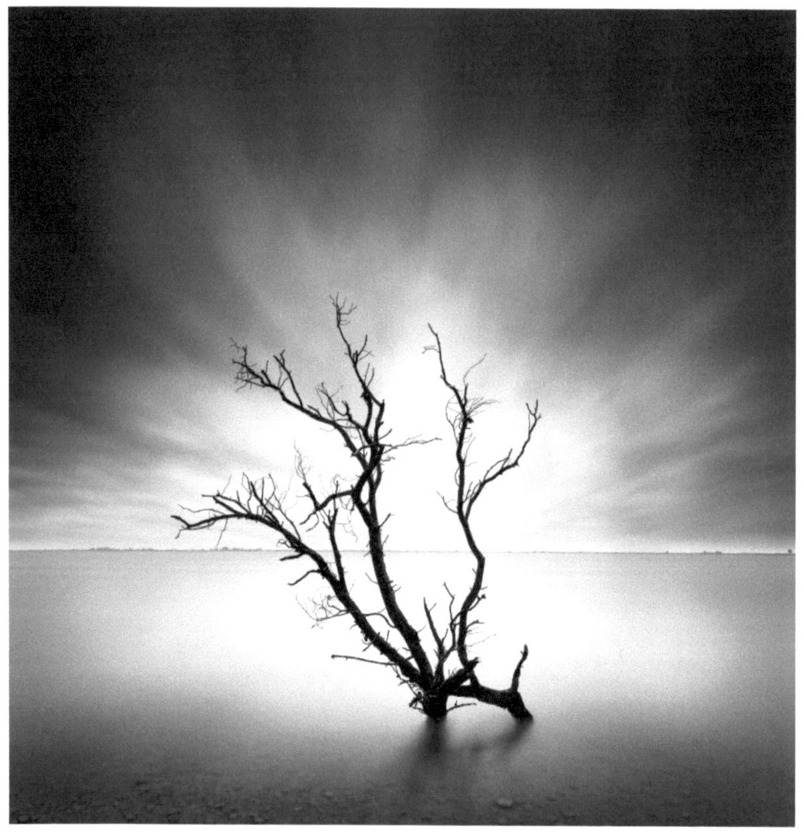

Genesis

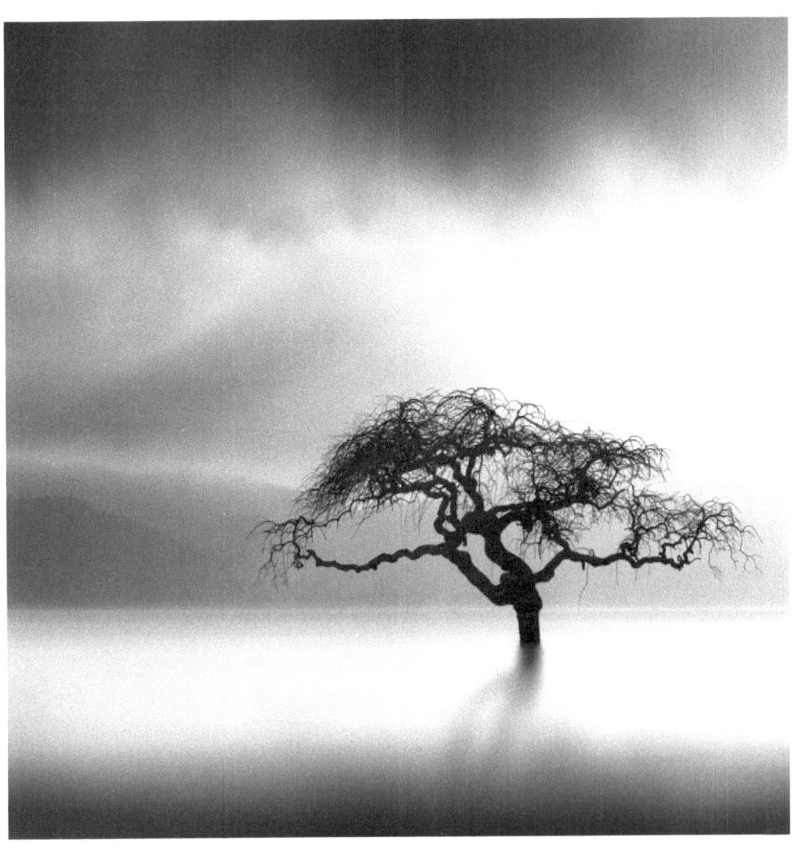

Illustration of Dreams

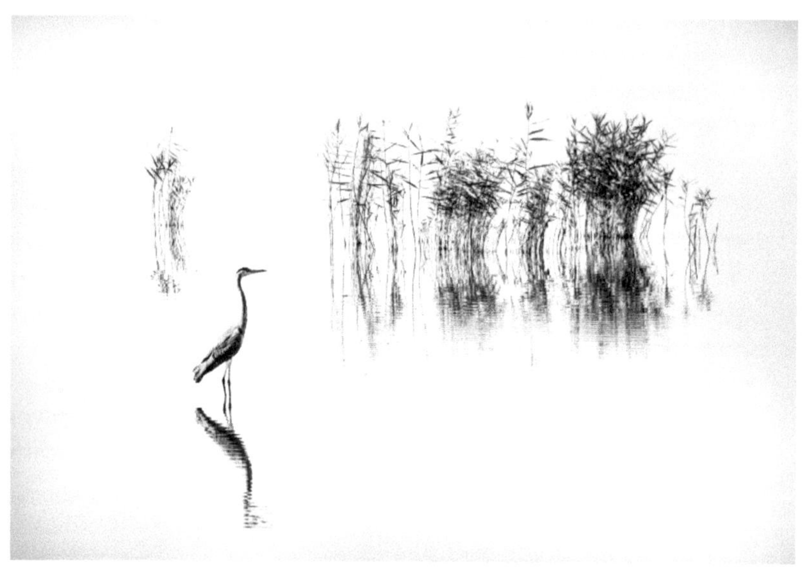

Lake Karla

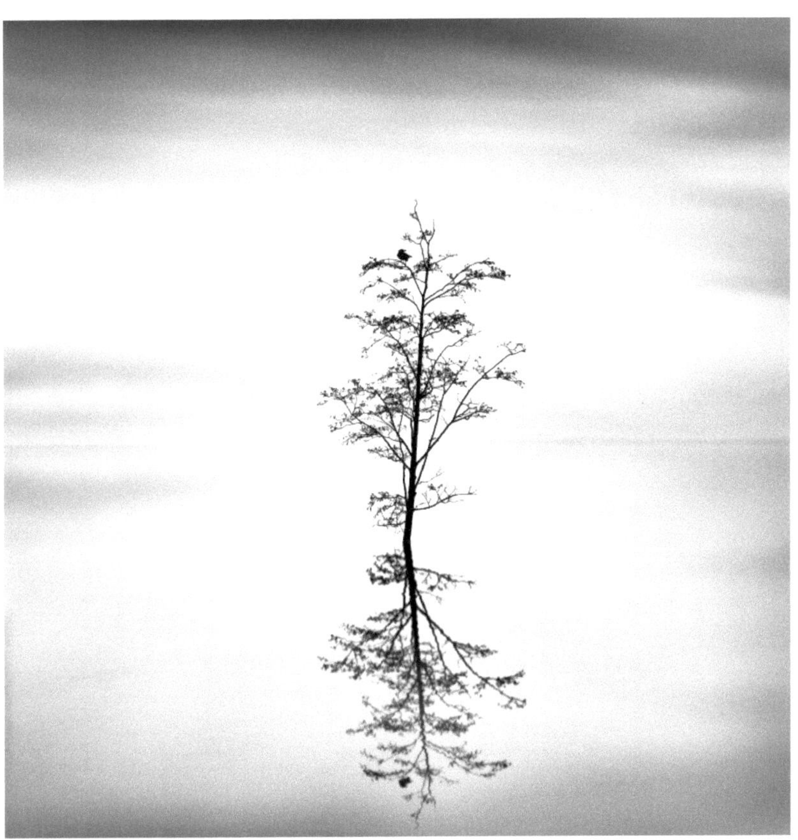

Lake Reflections

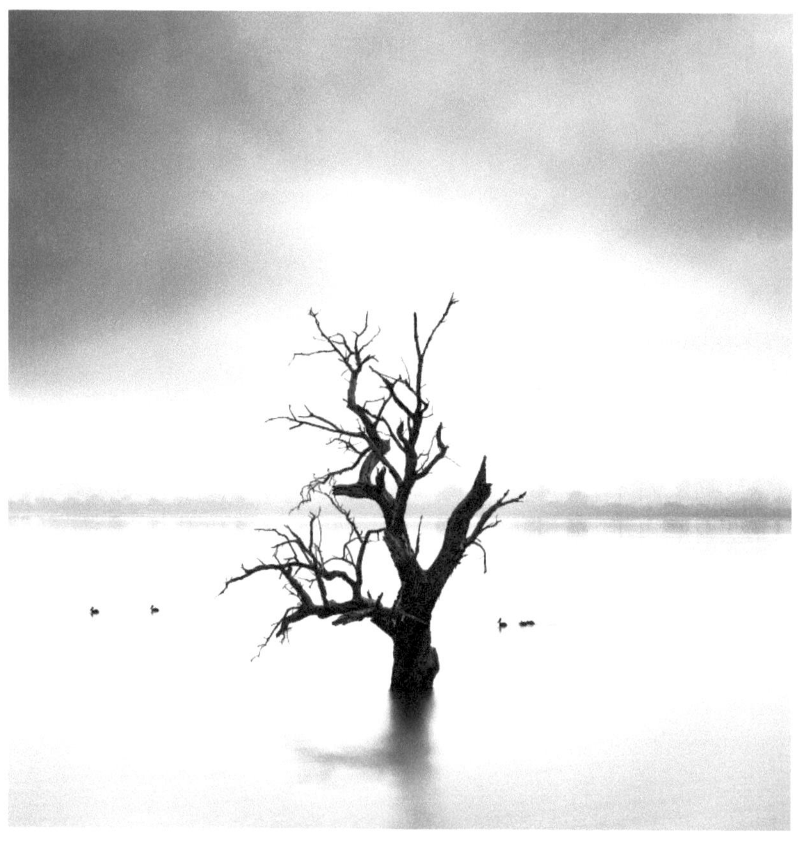

Land of Silence

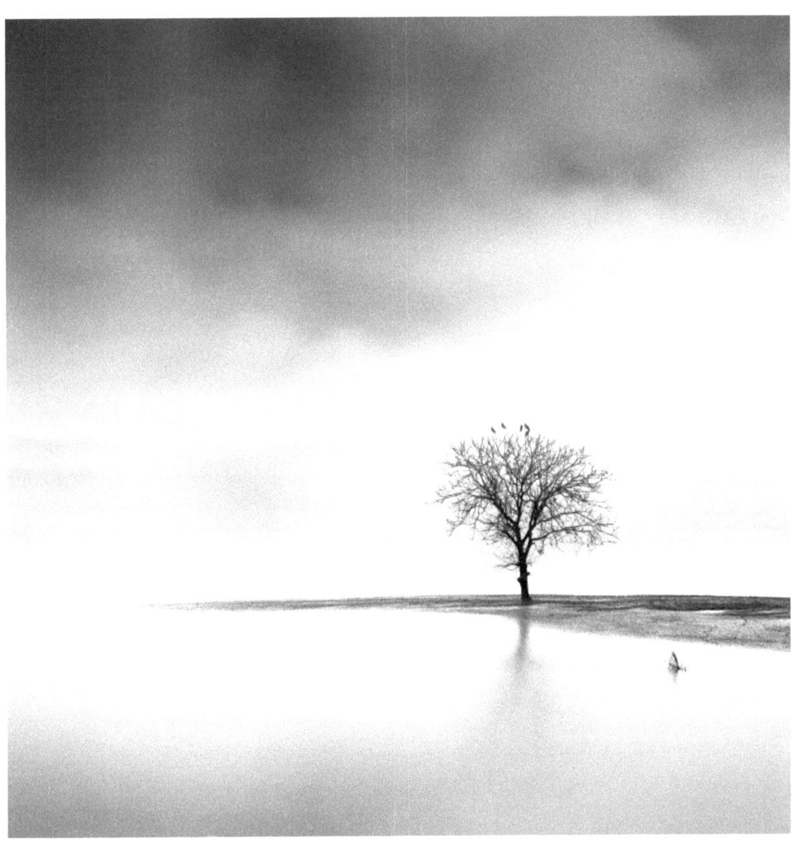

Landscape in the Mist

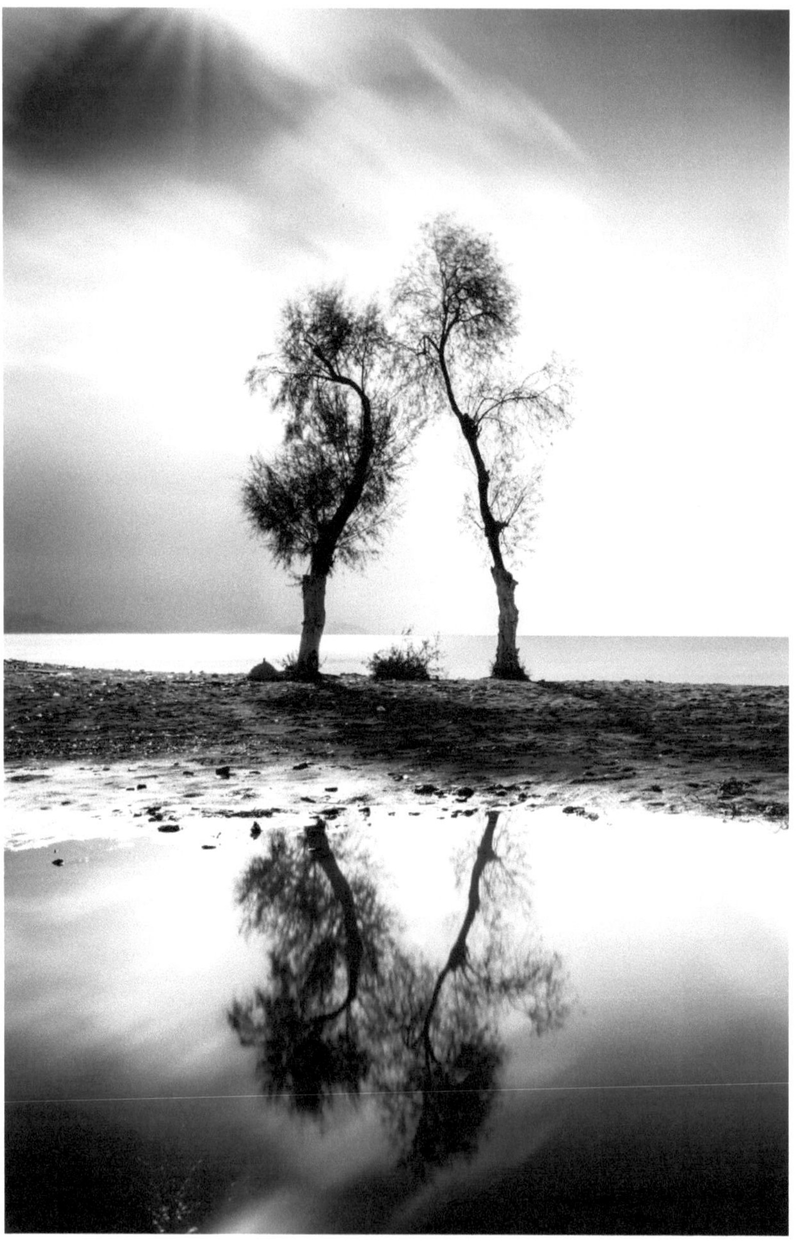

Lean on Me

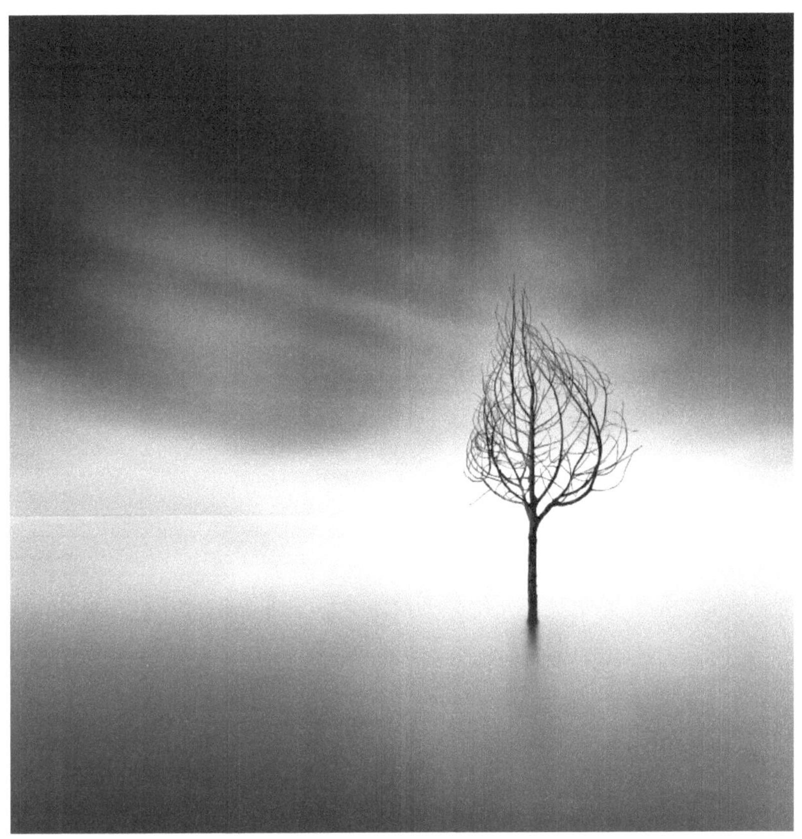

Like a Dream

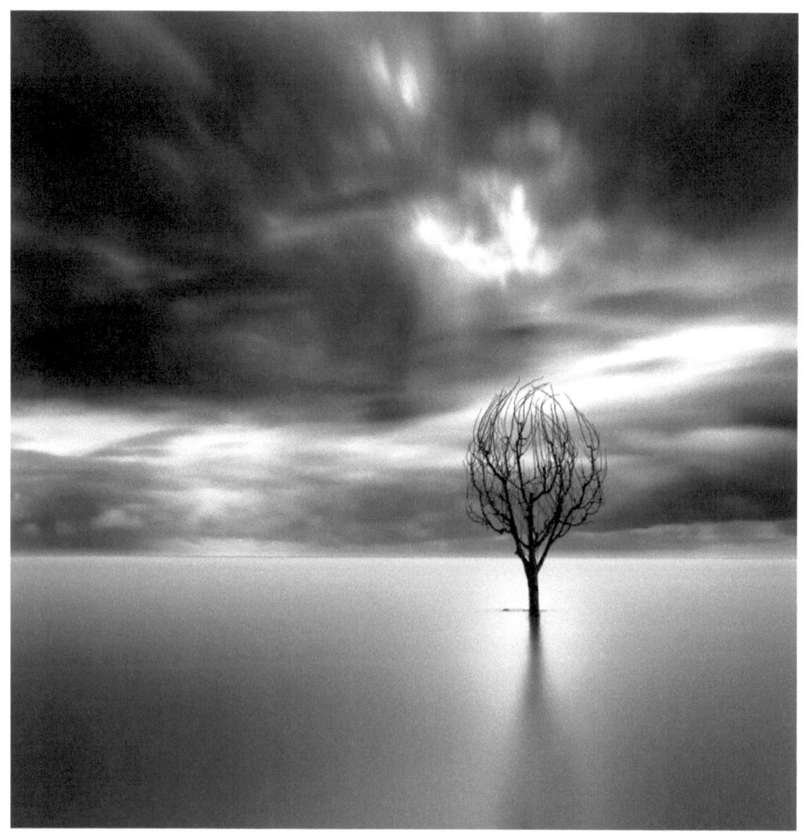

Lonely tree

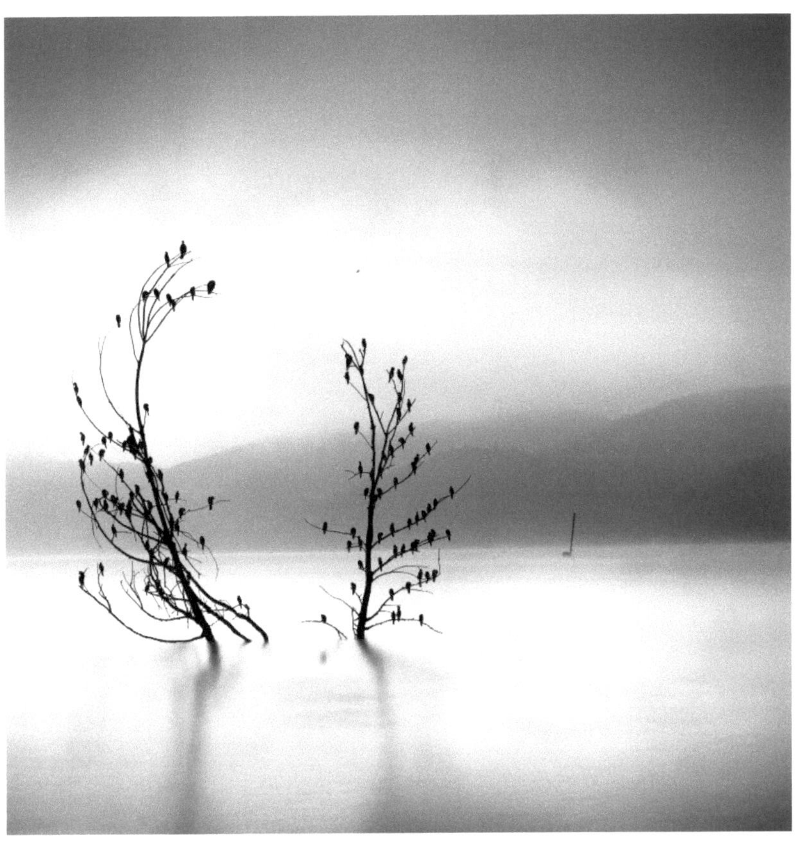

Ode to Joy

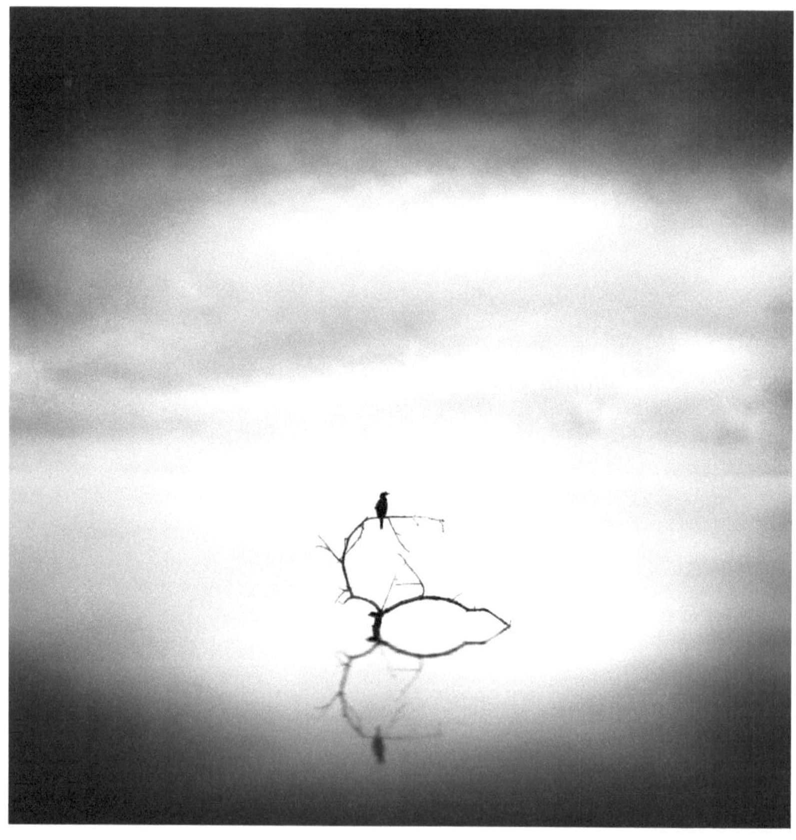

Poem for Loneliness

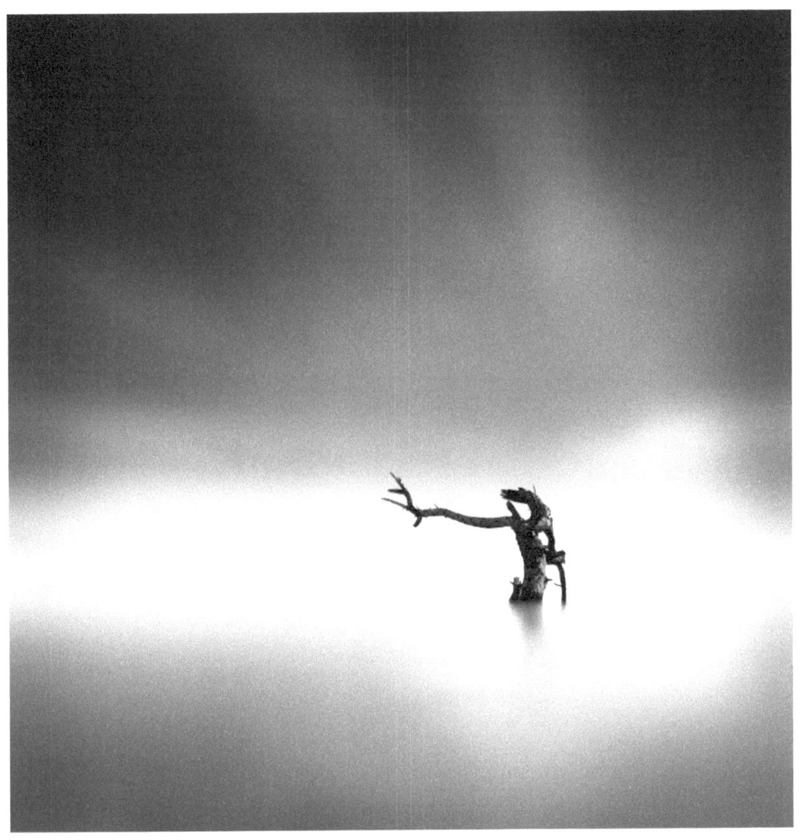

Pray

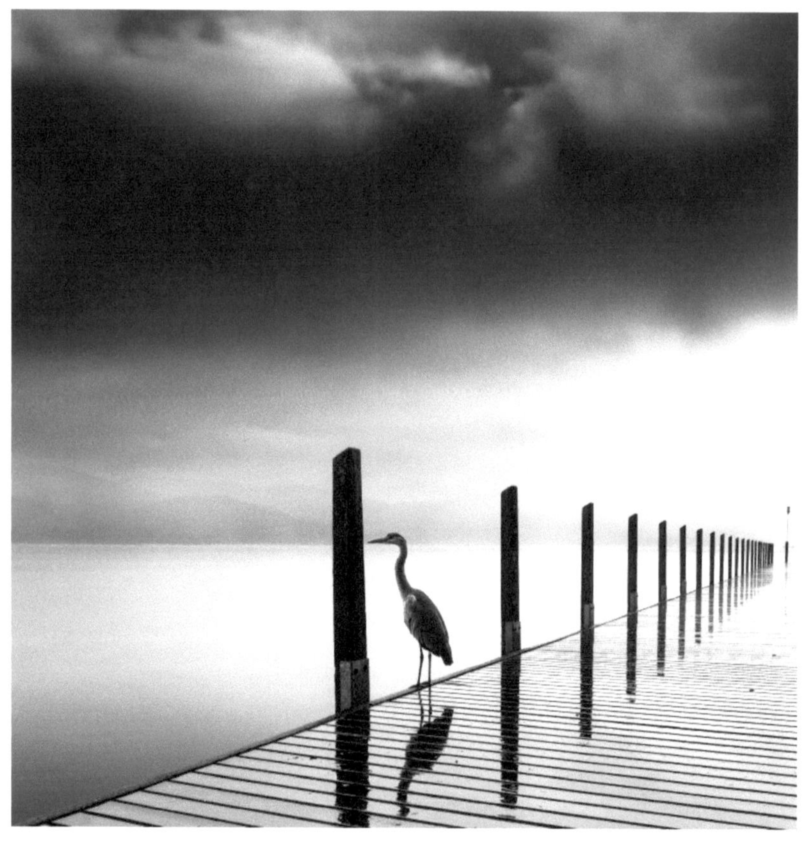

Rain Bird

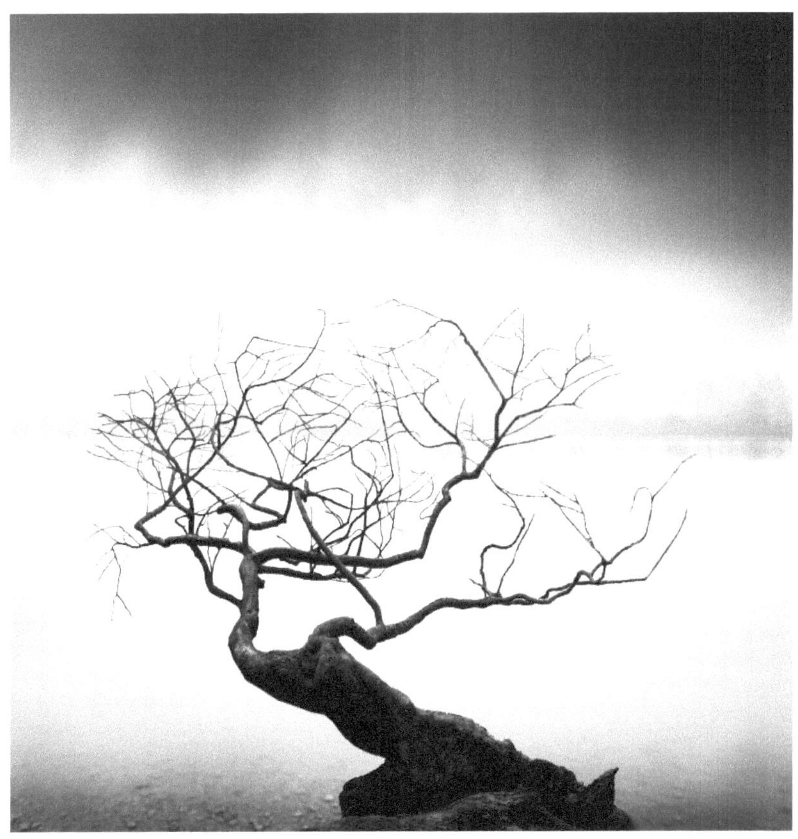

Root to Branches

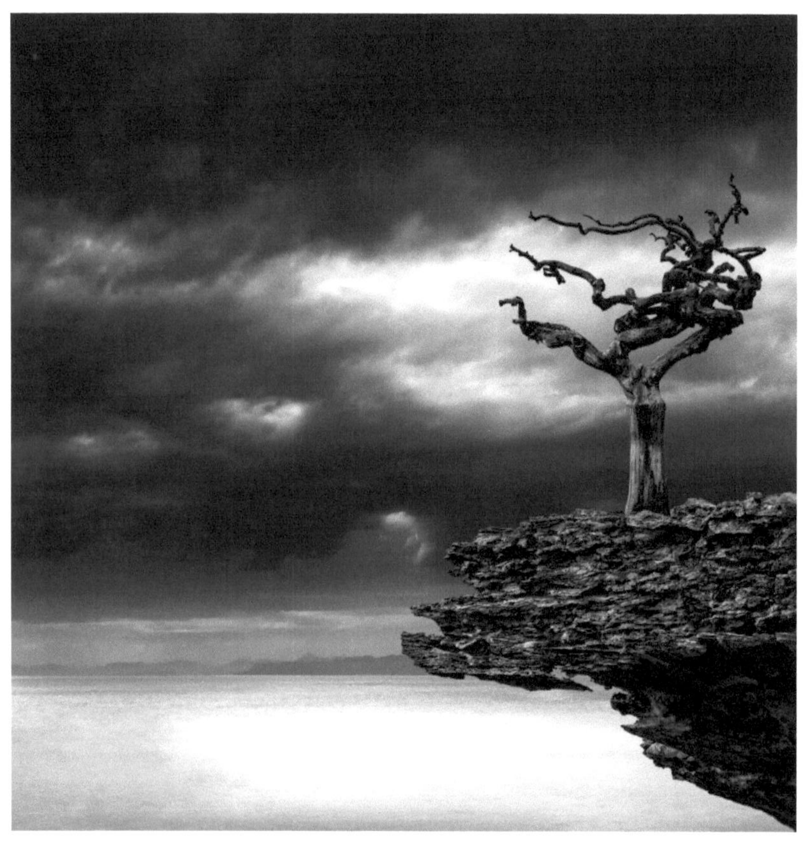

Ruler of the Seas

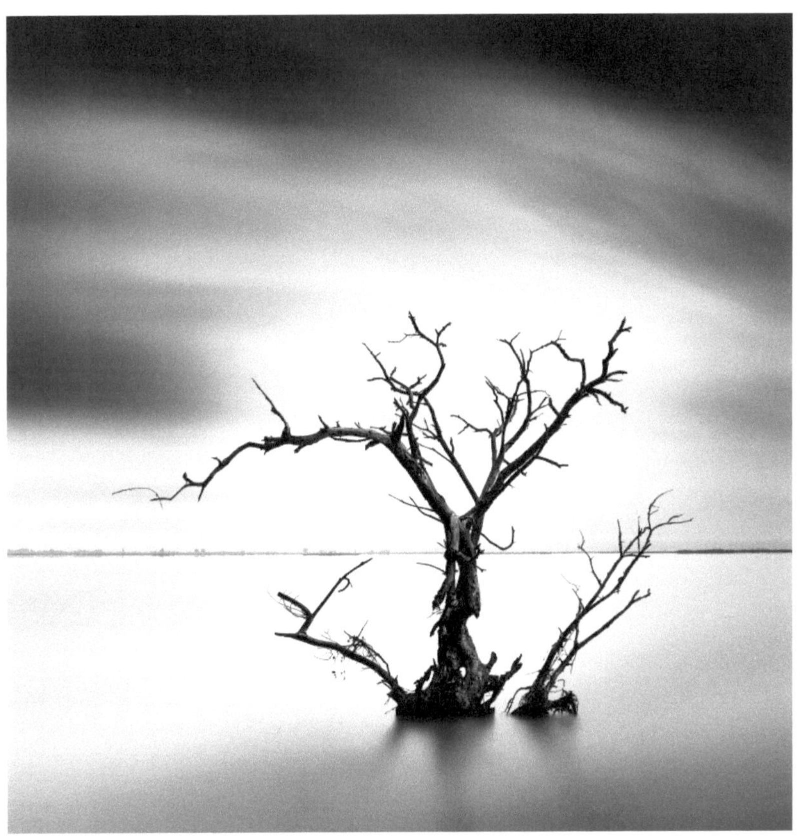

Sad And Beautiful World

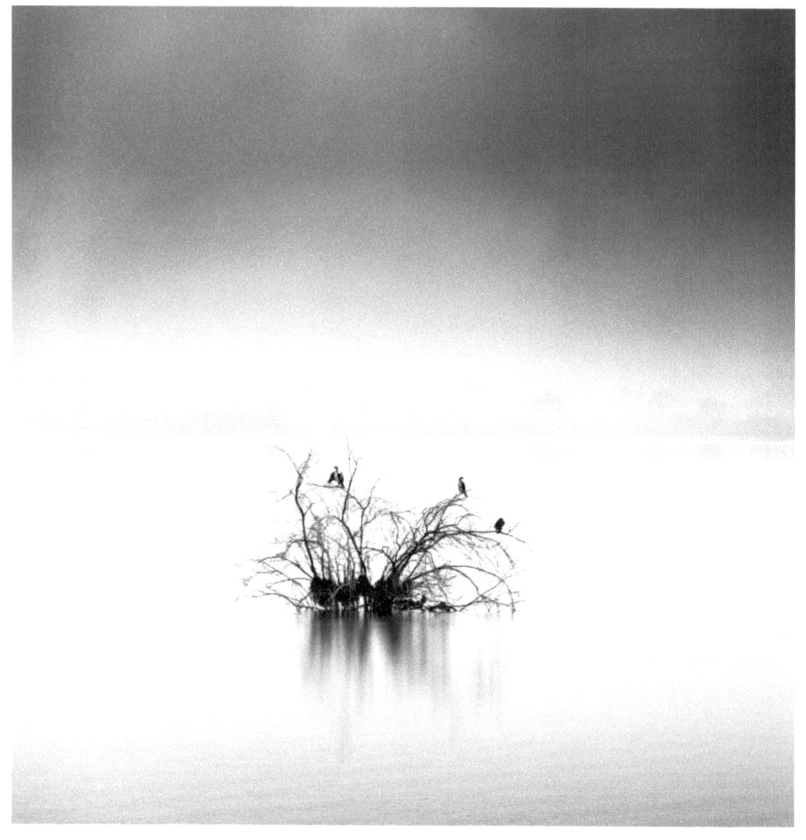

Silence

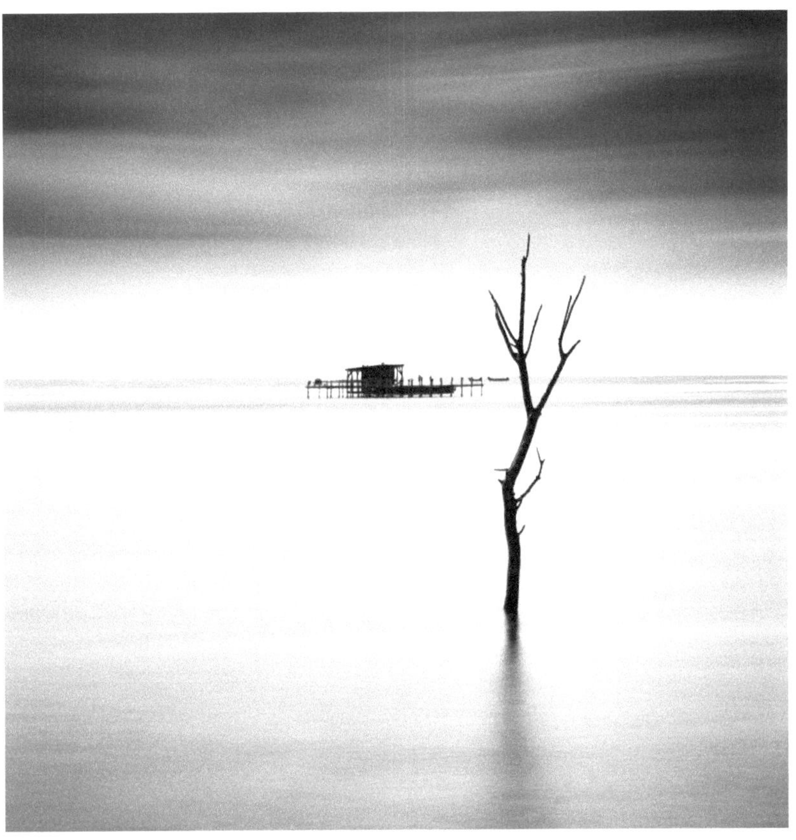

Silent Presence

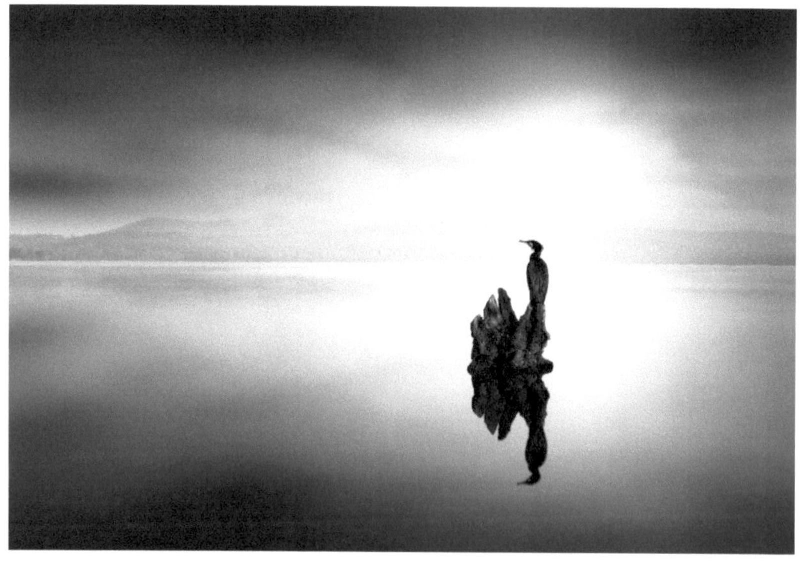

Solitary Life

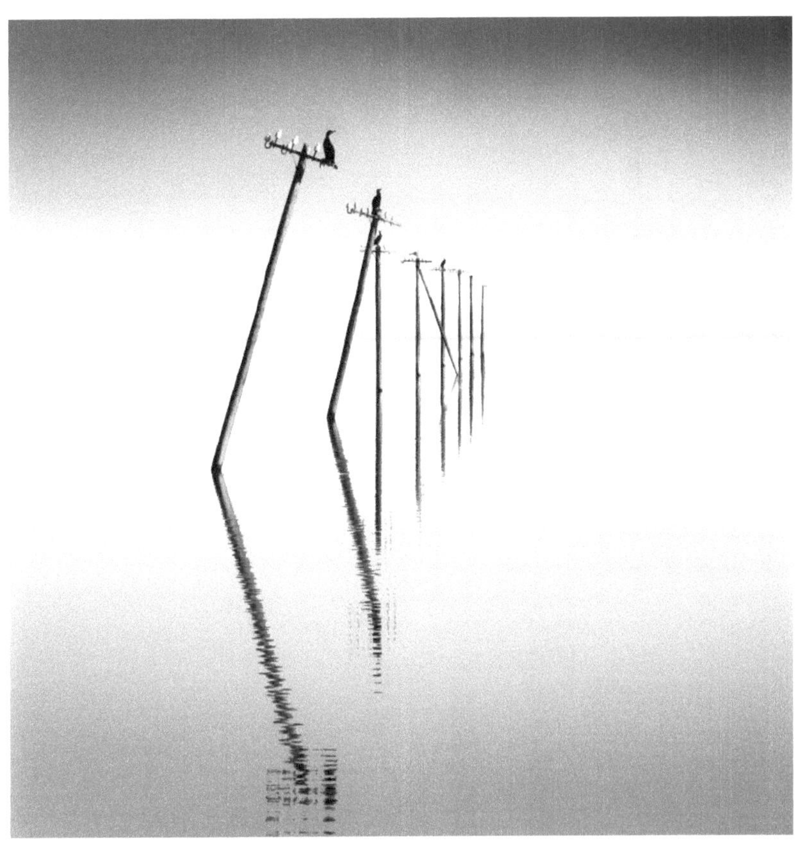

Surreal Reality

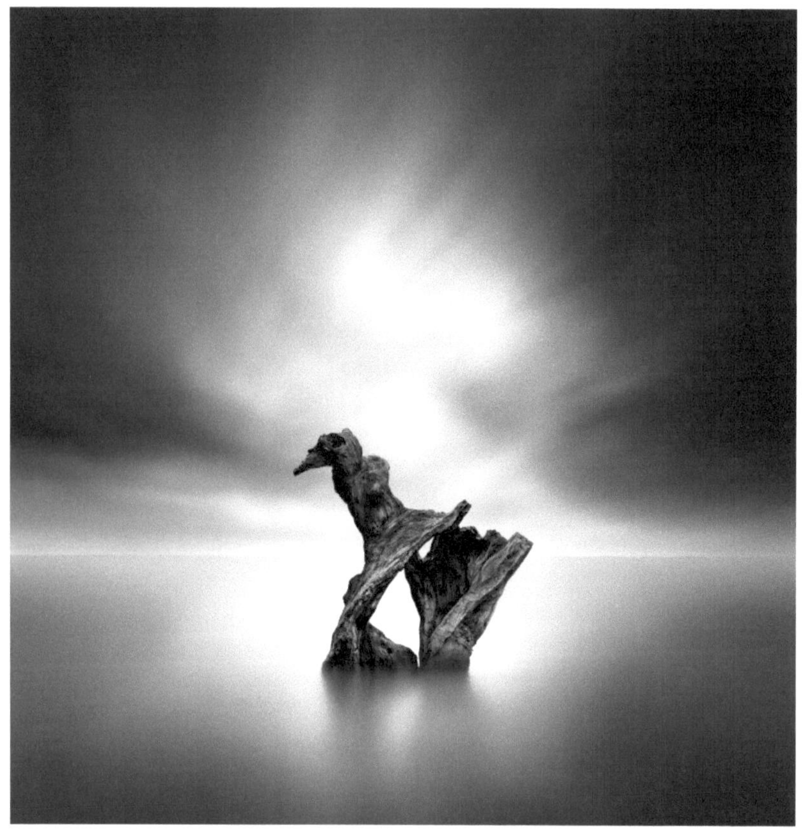

The Bird

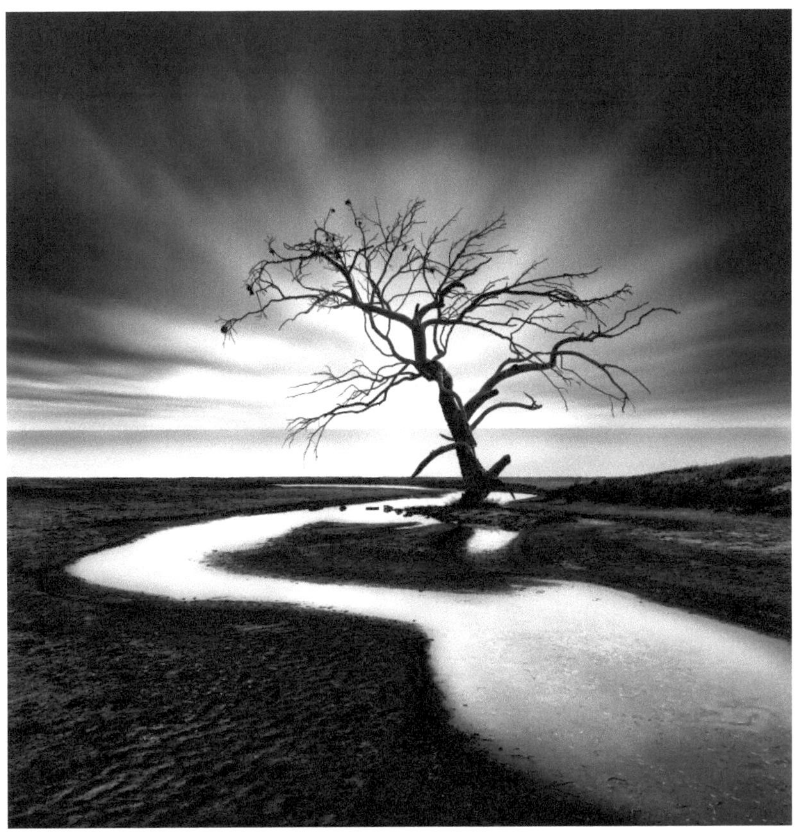

The Crying Tree

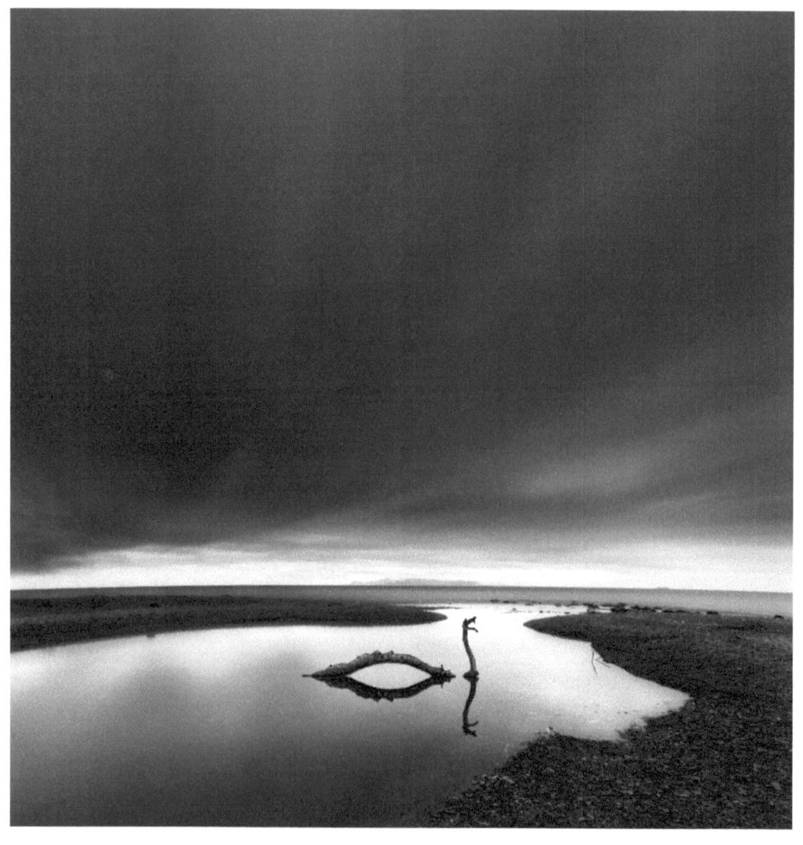

The Monster

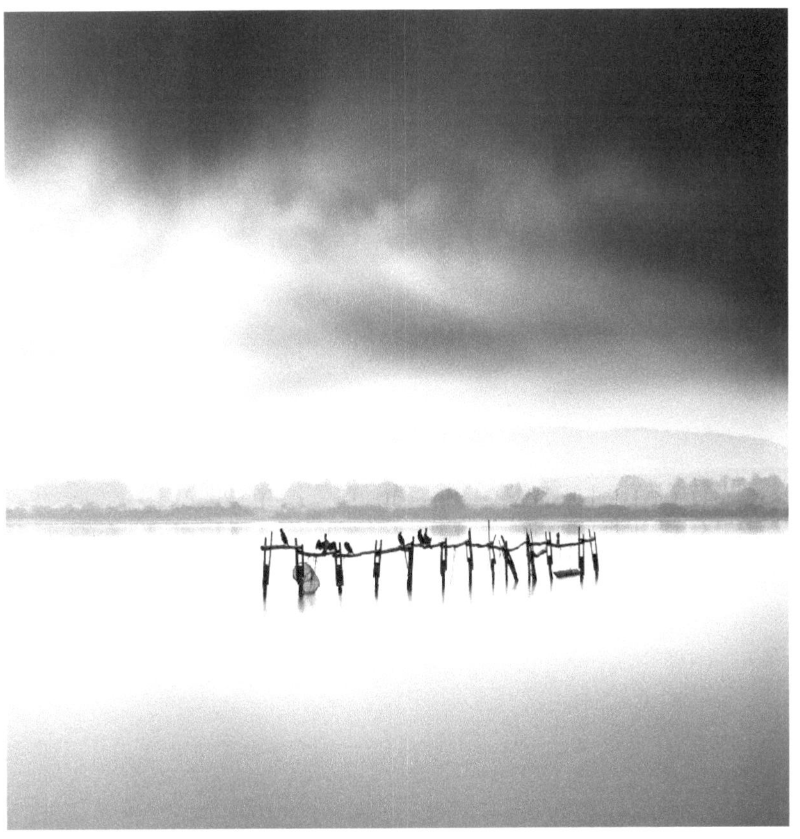

The Rain Song

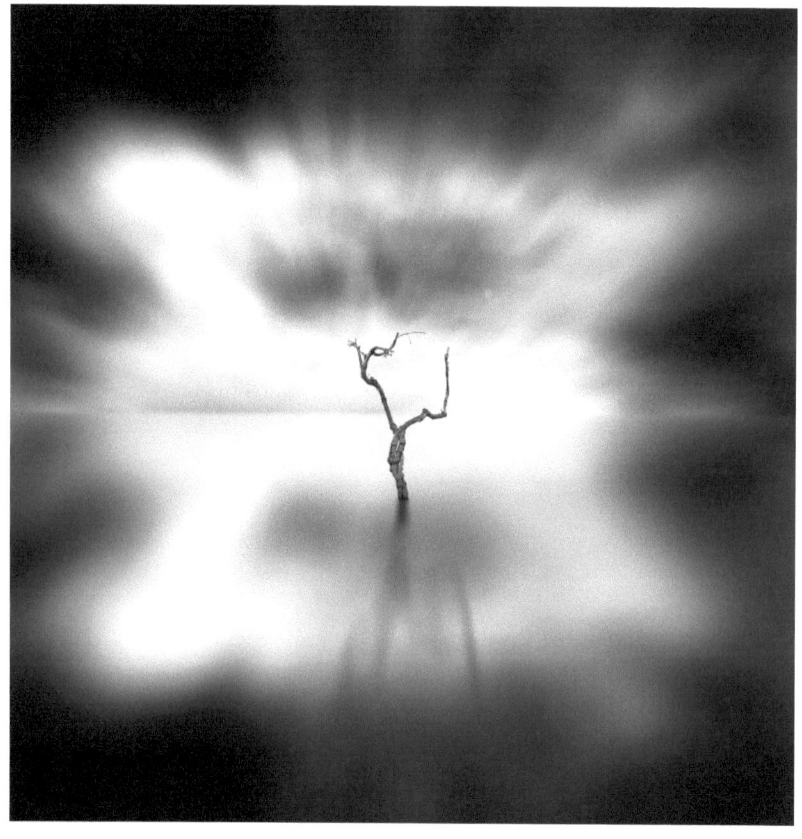

The Shape of Trees

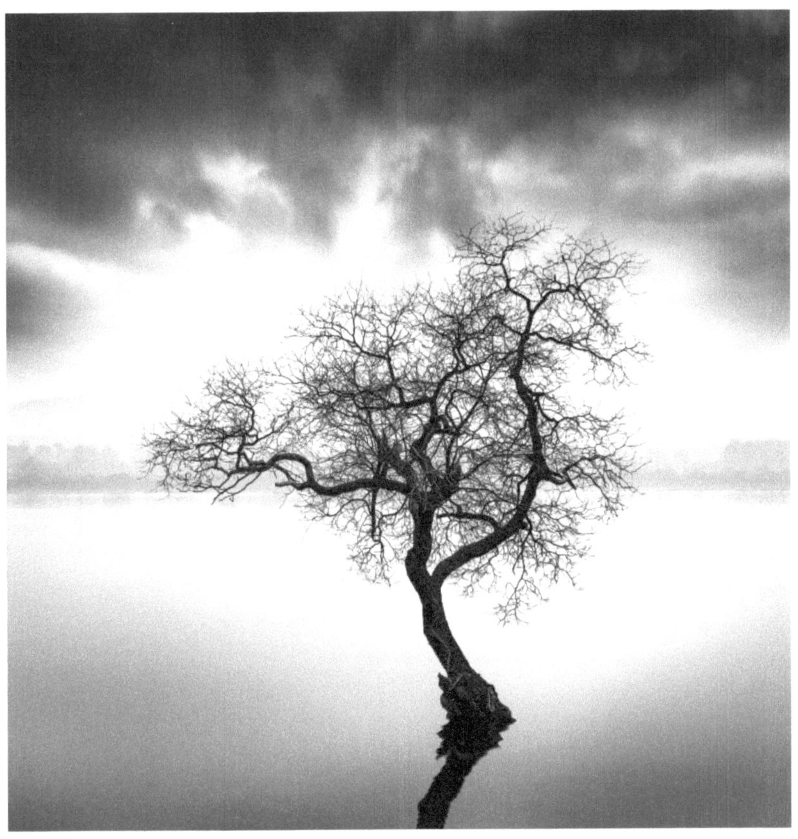

The Shape of Trees XX

Through The Eyes Of An Eagle

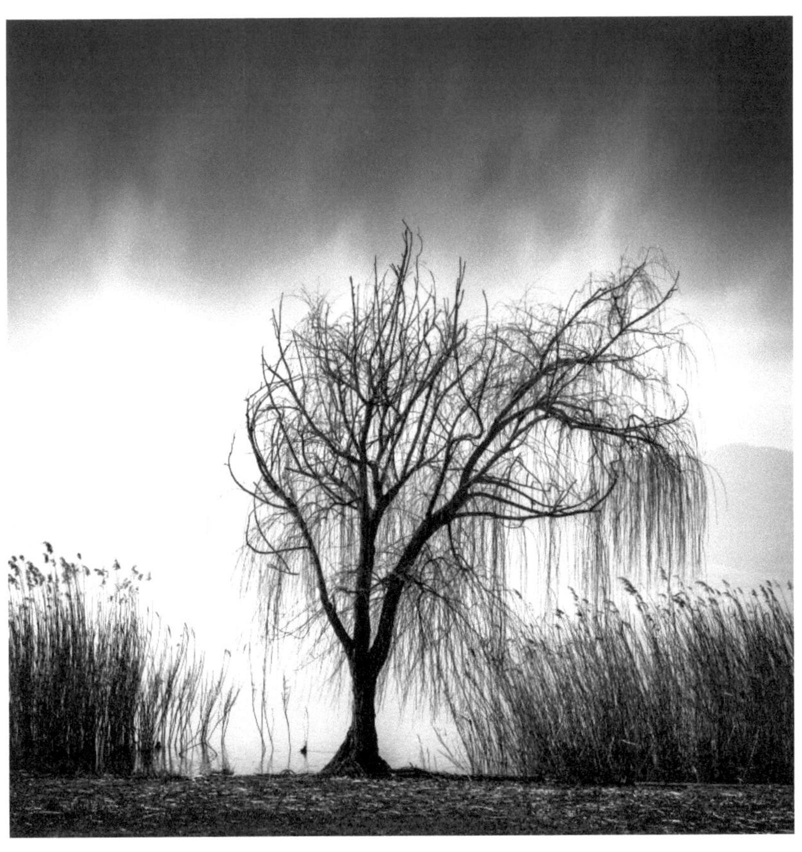

Weeping Willow

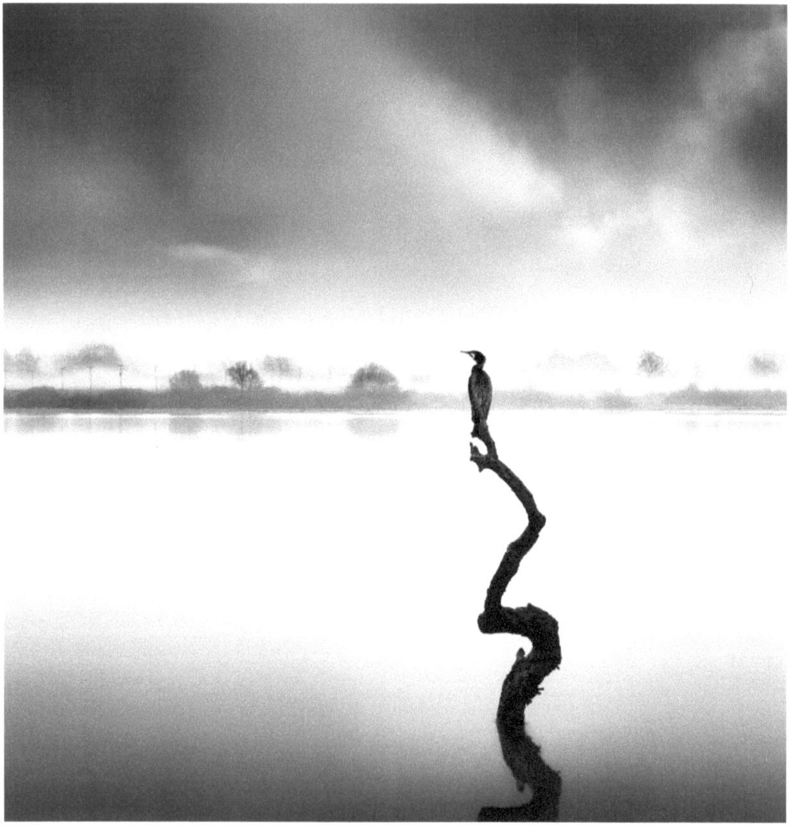

Whispers of Silence

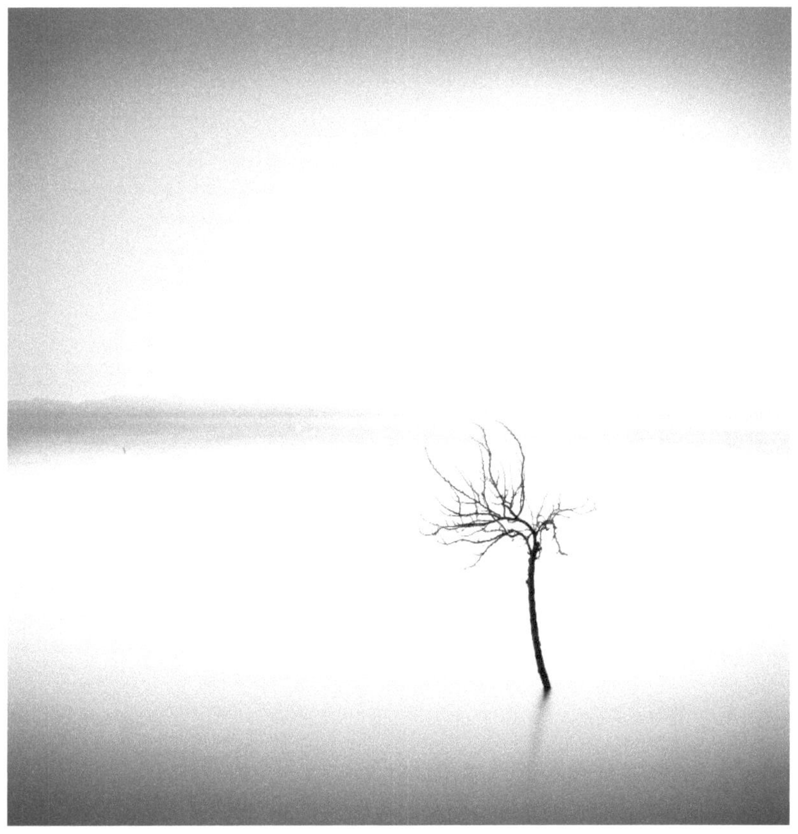

White World

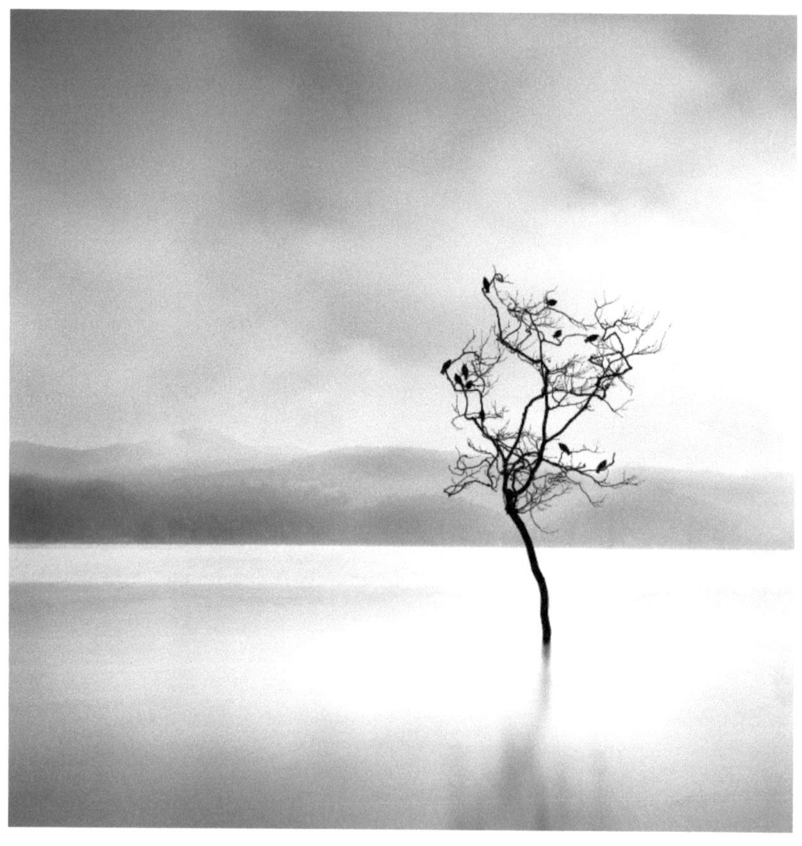

Winter Birds

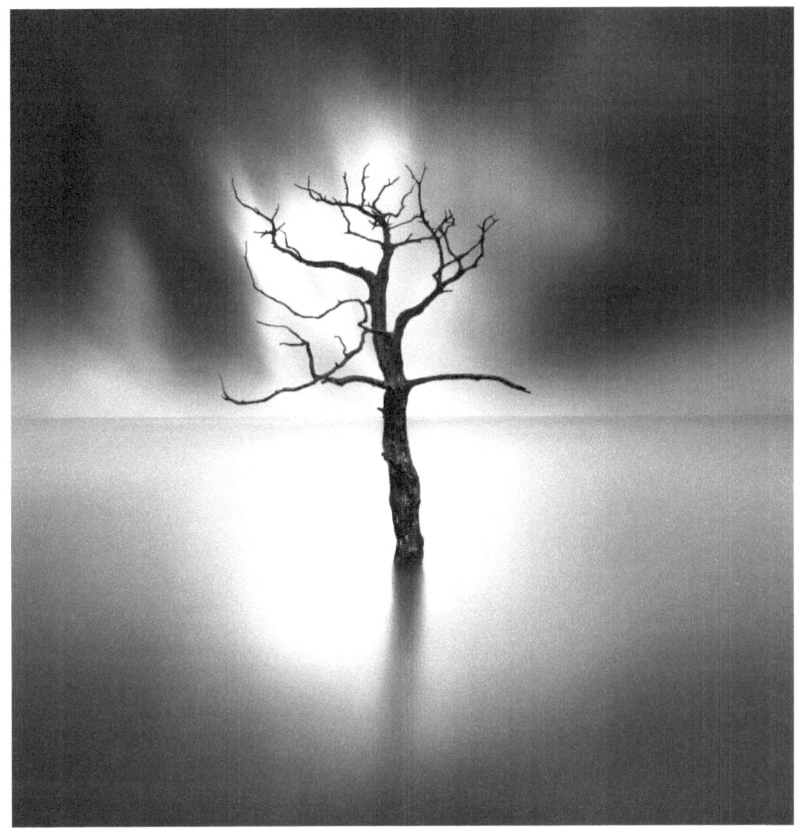

Withering Tree